Devil's Dictionary of Security Terms

RG Johnston

Saint Augustine(?) and the Devil
by Michael Pacher (1435-1498)

Back cover:
A portion of The *Laughing Cavalier* (1624)
by Frans Hals (1582-1666

Introduction

Terminology is not just pedantic semantics. It shapes and constrains our thinking. Security is a field that is especially plagued by sloppy terminology that gets in the way of critical thinking and precise communication. Thus, as a public service, this dictionary is here to clarify security terminology—with a nod and a wink to Ambrose Bierce (1842-1914?) who wrote the original *Devil's Dictionary* for everyday English.

Some of the definitions in this book may come across as a tad cynical, or even as reprehensible cheap-shots. But, hey, the truth is often ugly!

911: (1) The phone number you call after the criminals have left, or the fire is out. (2) The number to call to complain about potholes, barking dogs, and power outages.

Access Control: A technology or procedure that requires both employees and bad guys to jump through some hoops before being allowed in.

access: Entry privileges granted to anybody and everybody.

accountability: Scapegoating low-level employees.

actionable evidence: It doesn't *sound* like complete BS.

active measures: (1) Russian jargon for operations involving disinformation, manipulation of front organizations, agent-of-influence operations, forgeries, and counterfeiting. (2) US election campaigns.

active shooter: One who is energetic, in contrast to the lazy kind.

add on security: See **security.**

adequate security: Whatever we can afford or that has been budgeted.

adjudication: Making an official determination of whether hiring or retaining this loser would be blatantly gross negligence, or just arguably gross negligence.

administrative controls: Preventing administrators from screwing things up any more than necessary.

Advanced Encryption Standard (AES): A NIST-developed encryption algorithm that is considered much better than the Lame Ass Encryption Standard (LAES).

advanced persistent threat: (1) A buzzword to rationalize why our cyber security sucks. (2) The moniker we apply to any hackers 13-years or older.

adversary: A person who must overcome very minor adversities to defeat our security.

agent in place: A coworker.

agent of a foreign power: A coworker.

AI (artificial intelligence): The only kind of intelligence our organization is ever going to possess.

Air Force Office of Special Investigations (AFOSI): The U.S. Air Force's major investigative unit, called "special" because "retarded" is no longer politically correct.

airport screeners: TSA officers at the airport who confiscate your illegal drugs for their personal use.

All security devices, systems, and programs can be defeated: (1) But not ours. (2) An excuse to avoid having to strive for good security.

amateur: Anyone working in security.

annual security conference: Security professionals use company or government funds to gather in a dangerous and expensive city to drink too much and get swag from security vendors.

annunciator: (1) The company gossip. (2) A flashing light or acoustic siren called an "annunciator" so that the security monitoring company can charge more.

anomalies: Business as usual.

anomaly-based detection: Cutting way back on what has to be monitored by declaring all kinds of bizarre things as "normal".

anti-malware software: Software apps written in other countries by shady characters and foreign intelligence agencies.

armed security officer: A gun nut who makes everybody safer by only being allowed to carry around 1 loaded weapon at a time while on duty.

armed specialist: A security officer with a weapon who is

so dangerous that we only let them do one minor little
thing.

art forgery: art

ASIS International: A professional security organization
devoted to things "As Is", confusingly trying to be both
American and International.

asset: (1) Some piece of crap or other we are supposed to
protect. (2) Somebody we blackmailed into spying for us.

asymmetric threat: Pretty much any threat because the
competence of the bad guys greatly exceeds that of the good
guys.

Attaché: A diplomat or military official assigned to a US
overseas embassy who is too annoying or too incompetent
to keep in the USA.

audit log: (1) A pointless record of our pointless **audit**. (2)
A largely unintelligible, easily-tampered with, record of
computer activity.

audit trail: A largely unintelligible, easily-tampered with,
record of computer activity.

audit: See **security audit**.

auditor: See **security auditor**.

auditor: See **security auditor.**

augmented reality: The BS that security managers tell senior executives.

authentication: (1) Getting fooled into thinking some person, document, or thing is legitimate. (2) **Security Theater**.

authorized vendor: The vendor has friends inside the government.

automated password generator: An unsecured algorithm produces passwords that cannot be remembered.

automatic vehicle gate: Security hardware that keeps car insurance companies busy.

awarding contracts: Corruption, bribery, and malfeasance.

***** **B**

background check: Finding out if the person we are going to hire no matter what has a lot of speeding tickets.

background investigation: A **background check** called an "investigation" to give the misleading impression that it is thorough.

backup: To make an exact copy of all the malware on your computer.

bail: A strategy for keeping poor people and minorities in jail.

bank theft: Crimes committed by banks.

banner: An annoying, nonsensical message that appears on the computer screen when someone logs in.

bar code: (1) A kind of trivially counterfeited, not-very-unique product identifier or **tag**. (2) No shooting off firearms in the tavern.

barrier seal: A combination lock and seal that confuses everybody.

baseline security: Whatever security we have now, or can afford.

battery backup: A dead battery.

behavioral observation: People who can't win a hand of poker use scientifically invalid methods to try to spot criminals and terrorists by how they look.

behavioral science consultant: A supposed **expert** in behavioral science, mental health, psychiatry, or psychology who lost their medical license, couldn't get tenure, or the job at the strip mall just isn't very fulfilling anymore.

(the) best and the brightest: The people who wouldn't want to work here.

best practice: Those guys don't know what the hell they are doing either, but at least they seem confident.

big data: Rummaging around in terabytes of meaningless, random data so we look busy and profound.

bigot list: The people you can safely share racist or sexist jokes with.

bike lock: A **lock** meant to keep people from stealing the bicycle stand.

bill of lading: See **freight bill of lading (BOL).**

biometric verification vs. identification: You tell us who you are first, before we calculate who you are.

biometric: (1) A method for identifying you or verifying your identity, with the prefix "bi" because there are probably at least 2 copies of your biometric signature: one that is you and an identical counterfeit copy carried around by bad guys. (2) An access control device with no built-in security that it trivial to tamper with or spoof.

blacklist: (1) A list of the email addresses for citizens, watchdogs, and journalists who ask embarrassing questions. (2) A list of totalitarian regimes who have failed to pay illegal campaign contributions to our campaign.

blind shipment: (1) The **shipper** and receiver do not know the identity of each other, e.g., Amazon. (2) Any shipment that the **carrier** screwed up.

blister pack: Tamper detection **Security Theater** that gives the consumer blisters when trying to get the pills out.

block cipher: Short for blockhead cipher.

blown: To have one's secret cover outed, usually by a political hack or member of Congress.

blue team: The group of security professionals who feel sad about how easily the red team's mock attacks defeated our security.

bodyguard: A security professional who will stand guard over your body after you are killed.

bomb threat checklist: (1) A list of which high-level executives need to be gotten out of the building first when a bomb threat is called in. (2) A prioritized list of our security hardware and systems that are most likely to spontaneously explode.

bona fides: The determination that a person has completely fooled us regarding their honesty, sincerity, and **integrity**.

botnet: A network of zombie computers, e.g., Twitter, Facebook, Instagram, or TikTok.

brainstorming session: A person of authority running the meeting shoots down all ideas offered and yells at group members about how stupid they and their thinking are.

brand protection: (1) Attempting to prevent harm to the reputation of a company not caused by the company itself. (2) Using legal and customs means to prevent counterfeiters from making cheaper and higher quality versions of our company's product.

brief encounter: Recruitment of an **asset** where the underwear comes off.

bring your own device (BYOD): A company's cyber security policy that allows employees to use their own pornography-laden, malware-infested personal computer for official business instead of the company's pornography-laden, malware-infested computers.

broken seal: A **seal.**

brute force password attack: Guessing "12345678", "password", "eatme", etc.

buddy tag: A **Security Theater tag** that is so easy to use that it is your friend.

budget: How much money we have to waste.

bug: (1) A surreptitious listening device. (2) 50% of our software code.

burden of proof: It's a whole lot of work to find proof.

burglar alarm: Security devices that burglars may or may not want to bother turning off before burglarizing.

burglar resistant glass: Window panes that are difficult to steal.

business case for security: BS about why we need more money for **security.**

business continuity plan: Making sure that, after a catastrophe, senior executives still get paid.

business impact analysis: Fraudulently minimizing the severe damage to the business caused by our inept security.

***** **C***

cache: A type of money.

cancel code: A **PIN** that security officers, homeowners, and crooks use to turn off the burglar alarms, usually 1234 or 1111.

CAPTCHA: A series of image recognition tests designed to determine if you want into our web site badly enough to put up with the frustration of a whole bunch of ambiguous, eye-straining challenges. The acronym stands for "Completely Annoying Pathetic Turing test to tell Computers that Humans are complete Assholes".

car toss: (1) Secret hardware or information is tossed from a moving car. (2) An intelligence agent vomits in the car when he thinks about his career.

career criminal: A politician.

cargo security: Busy work that keeps the insurance company happy.

carjacking: Changing a flat tire.

carrier: (1) The cargo transport company that is bringing new viruses, bacteria, and pests into the country. (2) The company that damages your property in transit.

CARVER Method: We carve up our complex security problem into 5 different categories to make it look like we have some kind of coherent method for allocating security resources.

case officer: A person in charge of a **case.** Short for "head case".

case: A current law enforcement investigation, intelligence activity, or security project assembles all relevant materials in one place so it can be quickly shredded for **plausible deniability** if things go south.

Cassandra: Any employee who offers a warning or suggestion about security.

catastrophic event: (1) We are out of donuts. (2) Our embezzlement or our incompetence in providing security has been discovered.

catfishing: Hanging out on your social media sites.

cause and effect: Two totally unrelated things.

CCTV (closed circuit television): A video system designated as "closed circuit" to distinguish it from broadcast TV, which the guys in the guard station are really watching.

Central Intelligence Agency (CIA): (1) An independent U.S. Government agency responsible for providing national security intelligence to senior U.S. policymakers that is ignored. (2) Keystone Kops do intelligence.

chain of custody: A piece of paper, never to be examined, on which arbitrary individuals illegibly scribble their initials or signature for the purpose of making it look like we have some kind of security procedure in place.

change blindness: Our unwillingness to see the need for changes to **security.**

Chief Information Officer (CISO): A security manager who guards information yet possesses very little.

Chief Security Officer (CSO): The manager we marginalize, under-fund, and then blame for security incidents.

cipher pad: See **one-time pad.**

ciphertext: An encrypted form of useless text.

civil liberties: We will be polite while we take liberties with your Constitutional rights.

clandestine: See **covert.**

classification guide: (1) A document that outlines in ambiguous language what might or might not be classified, depending on who you ask and how you interpret the language. (2) An official document that directly contradicts the analogous document prepared by a different government agency.

classification marking: Markings, applied to classified documents indicating their security level, that make things convenient for the bad guys.

Classified Information Spillage: lunch.

classified: (1) A prestige label for pointless data and projects that elevates their importance. (2) A way to prevent colleagues or the taxpayers from finding out what we are doing so we don't get embarrassed.

clear zone: An area outside a facility that is cleared of bushes, trees, and debris so that intruders can get their vehicles and equipment closer to the perimeter fence.

clearance: (1) Access to sensitive or classified information, granted to individuals who have totally fooled us as to their reliability and trustworthiness. (2) You are now cleared to snoop.

Cleared Contractor Facility: An industrial, educational, or commercial facility used for sensitive or classified government work that has marginally better security than your average Jack-in-the-Box fast food restaurant.

cleared contractor: A person given access to sensitive or classified information who works for a greedy company that only cares about making money, not the good of the nation.

cleared escort: A hooker with a security clearance.

(the) cloud: (a) Putting all our eggs in one basket. (b) When the Internet inevitably goes down, we can't do any work.

cloud security: An aspirational concept that some experts think might be achievable in the distant future (or not).

cognitive dissonance: Our security program.

cold crime scene: A blustery location of a crime.

color shifting: Our printing processes are so poor, you never know what color(s) you will end up with.

combination lock: A device that is a combination of a **lock** and a practical joke.

common failure mode: Different security hardware or software fails in the same way because it was designed by the same knuckleheads.

communications security (COMSEC): Measures to keep unauthorized persons from obtaining sensitive or classified information or telecommunications unless they try hard or are insiders.

community policing: The police harassing a particular

community.

company newsletter: Lies, spin, and propaganda put down in writing.

company values: Ethical principles that are called "values" because they are extremely valuable due to their scarcity inside our organization.

compliance-based security: (1) We cleverly switch our responsibility towards compliance, rather than security (which is hard). (2) An oxymoron related to **Security Theater**.

compromised: When you foolishly agreed to trade your time to your employer for money.

computer abuse: Battery committed against your computer out of frustration.

computer backup: It's always two steps forward and one step back.

computer forensics: Analyzing computer data to see if we can find enough flimsy evidence to name a scapegoat or convict a suspect who is a schmuck.

computer intrusion: (1) Bad guys gain unauthorized access to IT systems. (2) Computers keep interrupting productive work.

computer screen: A computer display perfectly positioned so that the boss can't see that you are asleep at your desk.

Cone of Silence: A small room for sensitive or classified conversations where there is so much deliberate background acoustical noise that nobody can make themselves understood.

conference speaker: (1) A person, discussing the obvious with excessive verbiage and unreadable PowerPoint slides in front of an audience. (2) Human melatonin.

confidence: over-confidence

confidential information: Information that almost everybody in the business and most bad guys know.

confidential source: Liar

confirmation bias / motivating reasoning: management

confirmation process: After some scumbag or other is nominated for a high-level position, we hold a hearing to find out if his racism, misogyny, and corruption can be ignored.

conflict of interest: Something else is more interesting.

consultant: (1) Someone who charges too much to spew out platitudes, vacuous suggestions, and common sense. (2) A person who couldn't hold down a real job.

contact memory button: See **Security Theater.**

container: A flimsy box with many holes and backdoors in it.

containerization: Shipping stuff in giant, unsecure sheet metal boxes that have been in countries that harbor terrorists and smugglers.

continuity of government: In the event of a national emergency, there is a coordinated effort within the US government's executive branch to shut down the government because we will have enough problems at the time as it is. (See **COVID-19 pandemic.**)

continuous quality improvement: We constantly strive to move from hopelessly incompetent security to merely mediocre security.

contract guard force: We can blame somebody else for the incompetence of the guards.

convergence: (1) Forcing the security thugs and security nerds to work together in hopes the two kinds of anti-social freaks will spend more time annoying each other than annoying our normal, psychologically well-adjusted employees. (2) People from the IT and the Security Departments now have even more issues to squabble over.

cookies: Tidbits of highly sensitive data conveniently

stored on your computer to aid malicious adversaries.

corona virus: See **COVID-19.**

corruption: What everybody else is getting away with.

counter-intelligence officer: Someone who doesn't want to hear about your security concerns because they will only make his job more difficult and get both of you in trouble.

counter-intelligence: Activities to gather information about, and undermine the activities of, whistle blowers, civil rights leaders, protesters, and anyone who criticizes a government policy.

counter-intelligence program: Our security awareness training is so awful, it insults everyone's intelligence.

counterfeit product: a product

countermeasure: A half-baked, ill-conceived, token attempt to deal with the gaping holes in our security.

courier: A person who can be trusted to carry sensitive or classified items or information to a recipient without stopping along the way at more than a half-dozen bars and sleazy hotels.

cover story: What you wrote on your employment application.

covert: My girlfriend/boyfriend only knows about 80% of it.

covert uv marking: (1) A super obvious, non-surreptitious pattern printed with an ink that fluoresces under ultraviolet light. (2) A **Security Theater** anti-theft or anti-counterfeiting tag.

COVID-19 pandemic: We have met the enemy and he is us.

COVID-19: See **inside threat.**

CPE credit = Continuing Professional Credit: A unit of credit you are awarded for keeping one window of your browser connected to an online webinar, while you shop and surf the Internet on the other open window.

CPP (Certified Protection Professional): (1) A security professional who has so much time on their hands, they can get certified. (2) A security professional who knows a tiny amount about a great number of things vaguely related to security management. (3) A security professional who charges extra.

crash barrier: The guard shack you keep running into.

credentials: Documents, status, or information granting access to sensitive or classified information that you have no need to see.

credit check: Obtaining massively inaccurate financial

information from credit agencies as part of a token
background check on an employee or potential employee.

**crime prevention through environmental design
(CPTED):** Designing buildings and modifying the local
environment in a manner than is not esthetically pleasing to
gang members.

criminal justice major: What to choose in college if
majoring in beach volleyball looks like too much effort.

criminal justice: (1) An ironic oxymoron. (2) Institutional
racism.

crisis management: Your job.

critical asset: A person with intelligence value who is
always complaining.

critical infrastructure: The rundown buildings and
facilities we are supposed to be protecting, called "critical"
for the same reason as a very sick person in the hospital.

critical technology: (1) Essential technologies and
products that are important for military purposes and must
be carefully protected to avoid financial harm to the bottom
line of defense contractors. (2) Hardware and software that
is called "critical" for the same reason as a very sick person
in the hospital. (3) Hardware and software that many
people are very critical of.

critical thinking: Not what we are paying you for.

cryptanalysis: It's cryptic what those math nerds do with their time.

custodian: The person responsible for shredding or erasing classified information if the Inspector General shows up.

(the) cyber challenge: IT geeks compete in chugging beer.

cyber crime: (1) Crime you brag about on the Internet. (2) 85% of all email and web sites.

cyber security: Protecting 1's and 0's.

cyber warfare: iPhones versus Android.

cyberspace: A fantasy world where you are not a geek loser.

cybervetting: Checking blogs, social media sites, and other Internet sources to gather information on an employee or potential employee to determine if they are hot enough to date.

***** **D** ***

daemon: Old-fashioned spelling for "demon".

damage assessment: A determination, after the loss of classified information, about who we can blame and scapegoat.

damage to national security: This release of sensitive or classified information could affect our funding!

dark web: Facebook.

database: (1) A collection of confidential or classified information stored on an unencrypted laptop that gets left in an unlocked car, or at Starbucks. (2) The department secretary who is the only one who knows anything. (3) What neutralizes data acid.

data breach: (1) Bad guys steal computer data, called a "breach" to flatter ourselves that there was actually some kind of security wall or dam present in the first place that the bad guys had to make or find an opening in. (2) Just another day at the office.

data integrity: An aspirational goal for all your wrong data.

data leakage: working

data mining: Digging in a dark hole for something of value.

day zero: See **zero-day.**

deadly force: Routine police work.

debriefing: Formally interviewing a willing subject to see if there is anything that could possibly deflect criticism of our security.

debug: To fix the mistakes in software code, thus introducing new ones.

deception: (1) Just another day at the office. **(2)** Undoing ception.

decipher: Turning gibberish **ciphertext** into gibberish **plaintext.**

declassification: The acknowledgement by the U.S. government that certain information is completely worthless and not worth protecting, and that this was probably always the case.

decode: See **decipher.**

deep cover: We have undertaken substantial steps to hide our cover up.

defection: Changing employers for better pay.

Defense Courier Service (DCS): Federal Express.

defense in depth: See **layered security.**

defensible space: Designed physical space that can be defended from an architectural perspective.

Defensive Travel Security Briefing: Warnings about the risk of venereal disease from foreign travel.

degauss: Applying a reverse magnetic field to stored magnetic data so that it takes some effort for adversaries to reconstruct it.

deleted file: A file that is not deleted.

deliberate compromise: Trying to come to some consensus on what we will try to claim after our insiders screwed up and stupidly and inadvertently released sensitive or classified information.

Delphi Method: We're too lazy or cheap to do real research, so we assembled a bunch of old geezers who claim to know something about security and listened to them BS.

Denial of Service: Cutting off a client or customer for not paying his invoices.

Department of Energy (DOE): (1) The Keystone Kops oversee energy and research. (2) An ironically named

government agency given its lack of energy. (3) An
organization traditionally headed by an illiterate jackass
and/or political hack. (4) A government agency
headquartered in a building named after a Secretary of
Defense who went insane, appropriately designed in a
Brutalist architectural style.

Department of Homeland Security (DHS): (1) A large
government organization that keeps America safe by
separating babies and little kids from their families at the
border, threatening foreign visitors, and hassling air
travelers. (2) The Keystone Kops do security and
emergency response. (3) A major **insider threat**.

derivative classifier: Someone who has been given official
permission to wing it in deciding what is classified or not.

derogatory information: See **gossip**.

Design Basis Threat (DBT): (1) Magically, exactly the
magnitude of the threat that we fancifully believe our
security can handle. (2) Maybe if we string together 3
nouns without adjectives so that it sounds like gibberish, a
blatantly obvious concept will seem profound. (3) A rigged
way to "test" our security based on circular logic.

Deter, Detect, Delay: (1) A mantra indicating that we've
pretty much given up trying to have imaginative, proactive
security. (2) An excuse to avoid having to deal with the
insider threat (which is hard). (3) See **layered security**.

devil's advocate: The enemy of bad security and Security Theater who is mostly ignored.

digital voice alarm: A funny sounding artificial voice saying something unintelligible in an emergency.

diplomatic immunity: A status that permits you to do various crimes, including smuggling, terrorism, and ignoring parking tickets.

Director of National Intelligence (DNI): The principal adviser to the President, the National Security Council, and the Homeland Security Council who uses sock puppets and cartoon characters to dumb down intelligence findings.

dirty bomb: A weapon of mass destruction that wasn't obtained using ethical means.

discovery for litigation: Fishing expedition.

disgruntlement mitigation: (1) Retaliating against any employee who appears disgruntled. (2) How we mishandle employees who are no longer gruntled.

disinformation: Information released to dis people.

dispatch: Alerting the proper authorities within a few hours of an alarm.

displacement: Unethically driving bad guys to attack somebody else by installing a little half-ass security.

divided loyalties: married

division by zero: A frequent calculation in our software and security devices.

domain: A group of computers that all share the same serious security flaws.

domestic intelligence: Election campaign.

door magnetic tamper switch: A tamper switch that can be spoofed with a magnet.

Doppler motion detector: A security device that uses the Doppler Effect to not detect intruders.

dormant code: Most of the software products we put on the market.

drive-by attack: Your security is so poor, the adversaries don't even have to stop the car.

drug testing: Testing of an employee's urine undertaken with such poor security that it is actually a determination if the employee (1) is so high that he/she can't figure out how to cheat and (2) has coworkers or foreign agents who want him or her fired.

dual citizen: A schizophrenic with 2 personalities.

dual motion detector: Neither PIR nor microwave doppler technology give reliable enough intruder detection on their own, so we combine them because we don't have anything better.

dual technology: Incorporating a second technology to distract the end user from the inadequacies of the first technology, and from questioning the overall efficacy of the security product.

dual use: Technology that is as worthless for military applications as it is for non-military ones.

due diligence: Doing the minimum we can get away with and still avoid major jury awards.

dumpster diving: Looking for our lost sensitive documents in the garbage.

dunnage: Packing material used to support and protect cargo, and to hide the fact that a portion of the cargo has been stolen.

duress code: A special **PIN** that is entered into a security system by security guards in the field that generates an alarm at the central monitoring station, indicating they are out of coffee or donuts.

duty roster: A list of who is going to pretend to guard what and when, readily available to adversaries to tamper with.

dynamic threat assessment: A threat assessment that differs from usual threat assessments in that a bit of energy was put into it.

eCERT (electronic certification): Electronic documents sent for shipments from overseas that can assist law enforcement officials in their investigation after an act of smuggling, counterfeiting, or terrorism is accidently detected.

economic espionage: See **industrial espionage**.

effects-based security: Lacking any convincing evidence that our security makes any difference whatsoever, we use this term to imply that our security has some kind of impact on the risks we face.

eKey: An electronic key that is so poor, it rates below a grade of 'F'.

election integrity: (1) An oxymoron. (2) See **election security**.

election security: An oxymoron that refers to attempts to secure voting while using massively unsecure hardware, software, and procedures, overseen by wholly unreliable amateurs with little to no background checks, supervised by political hacks who don't think elections need security.

electronic seal: A type of tampering-indicating seal that frees up the seal inspector from having to worry about whether the seal was smashed open, if there is a large hole in the container, or if the door was ever closed.

embassy security: Marine guards stand watch to assure that the angry mobs storm the embassy walls in an orderly manner.

embedded system: (1) A product that incorporates computers or microprocessors that are buried as deep as possible inside the product in hopes that the end user won't discover the software bugs, security flaws, design blunders, and general incompetence. (2) A product that employs a computer or microprocessor dedicated to a specific task because the developer is not clever enough to write multi-tasking code. (3) A product that contains a computer (instead of a microcontroller) with way too much computing power for the relevant application—thus increasing marginal cost and opening up all kinds of unnecessary security vulnerabilities—because the developer is too lazy to develop an interface to the end user on a simple microcontroller.

emergency planning: Panic-mode planning because the higher-ups found out we don't have any security plans.

emergency response: The first swear words out of our mouth when it becomes clear our security has failed catastrophically.

emotional abuse: Another day at the office.

Employee Assistance Program (EAP): (1) HR thugs get

amusement from your personal difficulties. (2) Troubled employees self-identify to receive harassment and retaliation.

employee assurance program: A concerted effort to find evidence, any evidence at all, that the employee is not a homicidal maniac, drug dealer, or traitor.

employee grievance complaint process: Disgruntled employees self-identify to receive harassment and retaliation, thus better motivating them to do insider attacks.

employee morale: Something that HR and senior managers claim is sky-high but really doesn't exist.

encipher: Turning unintelligible text into even more unintelligible text.

enclave: A grouping of IT systems, all protected by the same bad security.

encode: See **encipher**.

encrypted network: A network that is so screwed up, the IT guys can't fix it.

encryption/data authentication/digital signatures: (1) Magical techniques for engendering irrational confidence in the security or veracity of data being exchanged between two devices or systems, each designed, constructed, programmed, owned, operated, controlled, and maintained by personnel who are utterly untrustworthy. (2) An imaginary silver bullet for dealing with any challenging security problem. (3) An excuse to avoid thinking critically about security.

end user: (1) The sucker or poor sap who buys/uses our security products. (2) The place or person where common sense, accountability, and any concept of security cease.

end-to-end encryption: Securely transmitting confidential information between two poorly secured locations, each manned by totally untrustworthy personnel.

engineer: A technical person who does not get **security.**

engineering controls: Preventing engineers from screwing things up any more than necessary.

enhanced interrogation: (1) Stopping just short of enhanced murder. (2) A vindication of Nietzsche's warning that if you fight monsters, you need to be careful not to become one.

Enterprise Risk Management: Entrepreneurs try to cash in on the fear of risks.

Enterprise Security: A job you don't want because if you beam down to the alien planet in your red shirt, you will get killed.

entropy: Our stock in trade.

ethical hacker: An attacker of computers or security who doesn't ridicule us about how stupid our **security** is.

ethics: Abstract notions of right and wrong that are relevant only to other people.

European Union: An oxymoron referring to a confederacy of arrogant, clueless bureaucrats.

event security: We'd better stop screwing around and get serious about security because now it is going to be highly visible.

evidence bag: See **Security Theater.**

evidence room: The police department Lost and Found.

evidence-based practice: If somebody on the Internet claims to be doing security a particular way, that is good enough for us.

exclusion area: A part of the facility where no work gets done.

Exclusionary Rule: Evidence can't be used in court if it is too stupid.

executive compensation: How much money senior level managers make which is proportional too how many friends they have on the Board.

executive protection: Wasting security resources on safeguarding worthless, high-level, asshole executives we'd be better off without, in order to feed their narcissism.

expert: A person with some specialized knowledge in a certain field who knows enough of what is really going on to be scared. (From P.J. Plauger.)

exploit: (1) A way for an adversary to take advantage of a vulnerability. (2) What a security manager or supervisor does to security employees. (3) Software that rips off customers.

export control: Preventing products and technologies that terrorists and adversarial nations already have from leaving the country.

*****F***

facial recognition: An automated biometric method for misidentifying people and discriminating against females and minorities.

facility management: facility mismanagement

facility security officer (FSO): (1) The guy who used to schedule the plumbers or deliver pizza who now is in charge of facility security. (2) A pre-arranged scapegoat for when the facility is inevitably breached or attacked.

fail safe: When the equipment inevitably fails, it might not blow up.

false acceptance rate (FAR): Our fraudulent claim about the acceptance rate.

false alarm: A frequent, reassuring indication that our security technology isn't completely non-functional.

false dispatch: See **dispatch**.

false rejection rate (FRR): Our fraudulent claim about the rejection rate.

Faraday bag: An electromagnetically shielded bag that allows certain government employees to shoplift from the Base Exchange without tripping the ant-theft **RFID** tags.

Faraday cage: A shielded metal vault where we lock up employees who are our worst security nightmares.

fault/event trees: (1) Formalized, logical approaches to confusing Safety and Product Reliability with Security. (2) We'd rather not have to think too profoundly or imaginatively about security.

FBI forensics: Lies or pseudo-scientific nonsense.

FDA approved tamper-evident packaging (TEP): The FDA glanced at your pharmaceuticals container and didn't see anything unfamiliar.

FDA approved: lame

federal air marshals: Creepy guys who stand out in a crowd, responsible for staring at the cockpit door during a flight. Also called, "chair marshals".

Federal Bureau of Investigation (FBI): The federal law enforcement agency that historically fakes forensics lab data, uses pseudo-scientific forensics methods, hassles and spies on civil rights leaders and protesters, and ignores terrorism intelligence from its own agents. Oh, and its first Director was a low-life, blackmailing, Constitution-ignoring racist, who some claim was a gay cross-dresser.

Federal Crime Insurance: Small businesses get insured for when federal employees cheat them.

Federal Grand Jury: A panel of rich people with lots of time on their hands who are tasked with determining if there is probable cause for a federal trial.

fence: What your employees do with the company property they steal.

file cabinet lock: A mechanism intended to keep file cabinet drawers from rolling open and whacking you in the head or knee.

fingerprint: A unique biological identifier possessed only by you and the bad guys who lifted yours and made a copy.

firewall: Hardware or software that is intended to block unauthorized access. Called a "firewall" because people will be fired when it is inevitably breached.

firmware: Badly written in-house software code for microcontrollers and microprocessors, developed by employees from our firm (which is why it is called "firmware".)

first responders: The people we send in first after a serious safety, security, or medical incident because the rest of us are selfish cowards.

fitness testing: (1) Making sure our frontline security officers can run significant distances because our official security vehicles and scooters are usually broken down. (2)

Checking in on an employee to see if he/she is sober enough to stand up on their own.

five W's and 1 H: Who, What, When, Where, Why, and How do we cover it up?

flap: An old-fashioned word for **tamper-indicating seals** or **tamper detection**; a corruption of the word "flop".

flash drive: A miniature storage device, called a flash drive because it allows adversaries to insert malware into a computer or steal sensitive computer data in a flash.

For Official Use Only (For OUO): A DoD designation for information left on tables in the foyer of hotel conference rooms and in public restrooms.

force-on-force attack: (1) An attack scenario based on the assumption that our major threat is a small band of stupid, unprepared adversaries who will mindlessly attack straight on, using force and zero insiders. (2) An attack using violence and weapons by a group of adversaries somehow always numbering less than the number our current security can purportedly handle. (3) An excuse to avoid having to deal with the **insider threat** (which is hard).

foreign contact: The foreign intelligence officer who is playing you.

four eyes (ACGU): (1) Australia, Canada, UK, and the US. (2) More specifically the glasses-wearing nerds who work for their intelligence agencies.

Fourth Amendment: A modification to the U.S. Constitution, added as an afterthought, that prohibits unreasonable searches and seizures, unless a judge or the police said it's ok.

frangible seal: A brittle, pretend **tamper-indicating seal** that rips apart with routine handling of the bottle or container.

freedom fighter: Someone who fights against freedom.

Freedom of Information Act (FOIA): Anybody (including hostile foreign powers) who is persistent and willing to file a lawsuit can request sensitive information from the U.S. government and get it 15+ years later.

freight bill of lading (BOL): A contract between a **carrier** and a **shipper** listing details about the shipment. From the old Scottish word "lading", meaning to lie.

frequency hopping: That damn communications hardware is acting up again.

full disk encryption: Encryption of a hard disk, enacted only once the disk is full.

functional manager: A **manager** who, atypically, actually has something to do.

fusion center: A focal point for sharing confusion and misinformation.

43

geofencing: Sounding an easily blocked or jammed alarm if cargo or a truck deviates from its intended route, and criminals haven't spoofed the **GPS** signal.

glass break sensor: A security device, typically mounted on the window, that can detect when intruders and burglars are amateur, ham-handed morons.

gossip: Informal chit-chat we use to determine what security products or services to buy, or who is reliable enough to share sensitive or classified information with.

Government Accountability Office (GAO): An investigative arm of congress that rarely holds the government accountable.

GPS tracking: Using **GPS** signals to kid yourself about where the cargo or truck might be.

GPS: A geo-location technology used for critical **security** applications that is easy to block, spoof, or jam.

graduated security: We apply several different levels of protection based on our whims, and because consistency is not our strong suit.

groupthink: See **security management**.

GSA security container: A certified filing cabinet for classified documents that nobody checks the back of to see if there is a hole.

guard station: The TV channel that the security guards like to watch the most while on duty.

guard: A kindly but addle-brained retired senior citizen, or a young drifter hoodlum who we hire by the hour to provide **Security Theater**.

hallways: Where we place **motion detectors**, even though intruders won't use the hallways.

hand geometry reader: A biometric access control device that lets you in based on the relative location of a few metal pins.

handcuffs: (1) See **Security Theater.** (2) Just more "security" hardware you can take home to spice things up the bedroom.

handwriting analysis: (1) A technique for deciding the identity of a person who hand wrote a document based on what results whoever is paying for the analysis wants. (2) A consultant who lost his or her Tarot cards.

hardened criminals: Crooks caught in security sticky foam.

hasp: The flimsy, poorly designed, and badly corroded hardware through which a lock or seal is passed.

head hunter: A police officer.

high security product: Not a high security product.

high security seal: (1) We and/or our customers don't really understand tamper detection. (2) An inane name for a **barrier seal**.

high technology: (1) It's expensive and doesn't work. (2) The owner's manual is badly written. (3) An excuse to stop thinking about security.

high-security fence: A security structure to keep out at least some of skateboarders and homeless people.

hinge: Hardware on a door that allows the door to swing open. Typically located on the outside, such as the same side of the door as the lock or seal.

HIPAA regulations: Scary sounding laws about medical privacy that nobody pays attention to.

hologram: A pretty, color-changing silvery sticker that hypnotizes the customer or shop clerk into thinking the product is authentic, whether it is or not.

homeland security: (1) What Beltway Bandits do. (2) Job security. (3) Snake oil or hype. (4) Fielding expensive high-tech hardware that doesn't work and hasn't been properly tested. (5) Spying on Americans, allies, world leaders, ex-spouses, and arbitrary foreigners. (6) A way around the 4th Amendment. (7) Protecting the USA. The country is called "homeland" and not "motherland" because we have enough similarities already with authoritarian regimes.

hostage situation: Your job.

hot wash: A review and debriefing immediately after an exercise or security test to figure out how we can cover up or spin the results.

HTTPS: The prefix to a secure URL that guarantees that the only people who will misuse your data are the recipient, or the hackers who have hijacked your computer.

human factors in security: (1) Computer scientists, mathematicians, and other techno-geeks with no understanding of the social sciences pretend they can model terrorist cells because they can't get funding to do real science or engineering. (2) Using psychological research to conclude that humans are morons.

Human Resources (HR): (1) Thugs who are the secret police, torturer, judge, jury, and executioner. (2) The greatest impeder of good security in our organization. (3) A good career path for those on the run from the War Crimes Commission.

HUMINT (Human Intelligence): An oxymoron that refers to getting information from people, usually by just asking them.

identity theft: Your creepy brother-in-law wants to be just like you.

identity-based access control: Access control based on the unconventional idea that we should know who we let have access.

impersonation: How you got your job.

impossible to defeat: Trivial to defeat.

inattentional blindness: Our **security.**

incident handling: Cover ups and scapegoating after a serious security incident.

incident management: Security professionals try to get their story straight before superiors show up.

incident response: Security professionals try to get their story straight before superiors show up.

incorrigible criminals: criminals

Independent Validation Authority: Clueless bureaucrats sent from Headquarters stumble through a review of security.

industrial espionage: (1) Capitalism. (2) The opposite of lazy espionage.

industry leader: More at fault for lousy security than almost anybody else.

industry standard: Badly done.

information security: Keeping necessary information about how to do a good job with security out of the hands of regular employees.

insanity defense: I hired that lawyer, so clearly I am nuts.

inside(r) threat: (1) We can't handle the external threats, so we'll threaten our employees as a distraction. (2) Our employees, contractors, consultants, vendors, and customers.

insurance: A tacit admission that our security sucks.

integrated system: Incompatible security hardware and software components are somehow made to work together without starting a fire.

integrity: (1) You are still in the game when things get gritty. (2) An amusing, old-fashioned idea. (3) Confidence that your garbage data haven't been tampered with.

intellectual property: Confidential, blatantly obvious

ideas and information that the Chinese government tells its many industrial spies not to bother with.

intelligence community: Pathetic losers who don't belong to any real community except through their work.

intelligence oversight: The process of assuring that the misdeeds and screwups of US intelligence agencies never come to light.

intelligence report: Classified BS.

intermodal shipment: Bad guys have many different opportunities to steal or tamper with the cargo.

internal security controls: Hardware, firmware, and software, provided by outsiders, that theoretically provide internal IT security.

internal security testing: (1) Testing our security inside the **security perimeter**, done by our own amateur insiders. (2) Just freewheeling some issues about security in our head.

International Atomic Energy Agency (IAEA): (1) An independent international agency whose function is to deny when countries are clearly violating international nuclear agreements. (2) Security Theater, but done under proper diplomatic protocols. (3) An organization of bureaucrats and safety experts who offer unwelcome and mundane suggestions to various nations about the security of their nuclear material. (4) An example of the adage that the only thing more screwed up than a government is an alliance of governments.

internet of things (IoT): All the security vulnerabilities, sleaze, and privacy violations of the Internet get combined with serious hardware security flaws and put inside devices that get distributed <u>everywhere</u>.

INTERPOL: Bureaucrats fight crime by writing memos and sending each other a lot of emails.

interrogation: Asking questions while lying, intimidating, or beating.

Intranet: A private, smaller version of the Internet with a proportionately slightly lower percentage of spam and porn content.

intruders: 1-5% of the people inside your facility at any given time.

intrusion detection device: Technology that only sounds an alarm when authorized personnel forget it is there and turned on.

intrusion detection system: A bunch of intrusion detection devices that don't work cooperatively very well.

intrusion: Access by unauthorized personnel that we unfortunately managed to detect despite our best efforts to stay blissfully ignorant.

inventory: A function that gets frequently confused with **security**, resulting in very poor security.

ISO 17712 Freight Seal Standard: People (who seem confused about what a tamper-indicating seal is) define simple-minded, arbitrary, and irrelevant "testing" standards for them.

IT support: Young, narcissistic, socially maladapted or psychologically unbalanced technicians who have unsupervised and unimpeded access to all our organization's classified/confidential information, PII, trade secrets, intellectual property, and cyber systems.

***** **J** **

jamming: (1) Interfering with the operation of a communication device by spreading jam all over the insides. (2) Playing music when you are supposed to be on guard duty.

JTAG: Diagnostic technology that makes it easier for bad guys to compromise security, electronics, and IT devices.

key control (encryption): Some cockamamie scheme or other for getting keys to only the authorized personnel.

key control (physical security): All the high-security keys are stored in 1 cabinet which can be easily picked open.

key: (1) An access-granting, small piece of brass with a morphology that can be read by a locksmith from across the parking lot in order to make a copy. (2) An easily guessed string of ASCII characters used for cryptographic **Security Theater**.

keyed alike: We screwed up and made every lock open with 1 key.

keyed different(ly): Somehow, none of our keys opens any of our locks.

keyless entry: If you poke the door with a credit card or paper clip, it will open.

keystroke monitoring: (1) What the bad guys are doing right now. (2) The employer monitors employees' computer keystrokes to make them feel creepy, paranoid, distrusted, and unable to vent, and also to encourage them to do their insider attacks without using their computer.

king pin lock: A **lock** to keep the king pin from getting stolen from the trailer.

knockoff: An unauthorized copy of a product that is less expensive and better made than the authentic product.

lanyard: A strangulation hazard used to hold an employee badge or security badge.

layered security (security in depth): (1) We're desperately hoping that multiple layers of lousy security will somehow magically add up to good security. (2) A security strategy that cannot stop an 82-year old nun trespassing at a nuclear plant. (3) An excuse to stop thinking profoundly about security.

leadership: (1) Management Theater. (2) A rare skill which, like integrity or character, cannot be taught. (3) Being an asshole.

legal counsel: Advice from company lawyers that the safest thing to do is not to do anything, ever.

level of protection: See **security level.**

liability: How likely you are to do something.

lifting: A nice, cost-saving feature where you can pick up a **tag** or **seal** and place it on something else without leaving any evidence.

line managers: The chain of managers above you, all who stick to the BS party line.

liveness detector: A security feature on a biometric access control device that verifies that one of the following is true: (1) a living human being is presenting the biometric signature or (2) bad guys—possibly high school students—have figured out how easy it is to spoof having a live human being present.

loading dock: (1) Where cargo is loaded, unloaded, and put on display for thieves to choose what grabs their fancy. (2) Much of **insider threat** all in one location.

lock box: (1) A steel box welded to the right hand door of a shipping container to protect the lock from direct attack for 4-5 seconds. (2) A plastic box with a combination containing the key to a house for sale for use by real estate agents. All possible combinations can be tried in under 2 minutes. (3) A locked metal box containing money that is easy to walk off with.

lock: Some hardware that delays unauthorized access by a few seconds and keeps out unresourceful youngsters.

locking bar: A hardened piece of hardware that forces cargo thieves to take 10 seconds to cut the lockrods or cut a hole in the container wall.

lockrods: Vertical tubes on a shipping container door that, along with cams, keep the doors from flying open during transit. To open the door, the lockrods are rotated using an attached handle, held on with a flimsy, badly corroded rivet. Typically, only the handle is locked or sealed because nobody wants to waste time inspecting the actual hardware that allows the door to open.

log-in procedure: You have to type "12345678" or "password".

logic bomb: Finally, our lack of logical reasoning about security has blown up in our face.

logic gate: A barrier to keep logic out.

loss event probability: The odds of theft, made up by guys so far removed from reality that they call it a "loss event".

loss prevention: Trying for more wins.

loyalty oath: A swear word uttered when your employee is extremely disloyal to you.

magnetic contact switch: See **Security Theater.**

magnetic remanence: All that ancient crappy data we have laying around on old hard disks.

magnetic strip: Stored 1's and 0's that are easily cloned.

magnetometer: A device to check if a person is carrying any refrigerator magnets.

male-dominated field of security: The main reason security isn't very good.

man trap: Technology at the access point to a sensitive or classified area that security guards routinely get stuck in.

man-in-the-middle attack: (1) A resourceful high school kid or the equivalent splices simple electronics into an internal or external communications channel in order to defeat, spoof, or hijack a security device or system. Often inserted at the input of LCD displays, the input or output of the keypad, or along the alarm line.

management: (1) Making arbitrary decisions based on arrogance, denial, wishful thinking, wrong assumptions, superficial impressions, flawed intuition, ego, and little or no relevant data. (2) A process needed because we didn't do a very good job of choosing employees to hire in the first place. (3) Mindless platitudes mixed with cognitive dissonance. (4) The blind leading the blind. (5) Telling the little people where to go and what to do. (6) A desk job for a bureaucrat, sociopath, asshole, and/or narcissist who possesses no discernible talent, knowledge, insight, intelligence, creativity, people skills, passion, commitment, common sense, or basic human decency.

manager: (1) A person with no obvious marketable skills who gets in the way of all the employees who do real work. (2) The knucklehead nephew or son-in-law of the CEO or HR Director.

Maslow: Abraham H. Maslow identified a hierarchy of human needs, none of which are being met by your job.

masquerading: What you are doing in your job, at least until they finally figure out you are a fraud.

material control and accountability (MC&A): Confusing inventory with **security** and safeguards.

material evidence: Actual relevant evidence of a crime, in contrast to the fanciful, made up evidence.

maximum tolerable downtime: Our current downtime.

MC&A: See **material control and accountability**.

McGregor's management theory: There are 2 kinds of approaches to supervising and managing: Theory Y and

Theory X, i.e., being an asshole.

meme: Your emails or security report.

mental illness: A necessary attribute to work in security, for the government, or as a law enforcement officer.

mentor: An older person who constrains a younger person from doing anything innovative or brilliant.

Message Authentication Code (MAC): A short piece of information that verifies bad guys have so infiltrated our organization that they can fake the MAC.

microcontroller: A microprocessor (integrated circuit) with memory that controls equipment and devices. Called "micro" because we have only a miniscule amount of control over it, and a miniscule understanding of how it works and its vulnerabilities.

microprinting: Ultra tiny printing intended as an anti-counterfeiting tag that is too tiny to be of any practical use in spotting counterfeits.

Miranda warning: The police warn someone they have stopped of his legal rights before shooting him or beating him up.

misnamed files: What is on your hard drive.

mission creep: The jerk you have to work with on this

project.

mission critical: Not mission critical.

mission statement: A short summary of how we squeeze money out of our naive customers.

mobile phone: A cell phone that criminals walk off with.

modus operandi (MO): Our simple-minded misunderstanding of how a criminal typically operates.

mole: (1) Your coworker. (2) Your sole biometric signature left that the adversaries have not yet stolen and counterfeited.

monoculture: The computer nerds get mononucleosis.

motion detector: (1) A device to detect if employees are inappropriately playing Frisbee or tossing around a nerf basketball when they should be working. (2) A device to determine when security guards have fallen asleep (3) An energy-saving device to automatically turn off the lights in the room when you are working. (4) The device that refuses to turn on the water in the restroom so you can wash your hands.

multiplexing: A whole lot of plexing.

museum security: Security measures that are so out of date that they are antiquities.

Myers-Briggs test: For when horoscopes give inconclusive results.

National Fire Protection Association (NFPA): A non-profit organization devoted to protecting fires.

National Intelligence Estimates: U.S. federal government documents that represent the authoritative assessment of the Director of National Intelligence (DNI) about particular national security issues. Called "estimates" because we are just winging it here.

National Nuclear Security Administration: (1) A government bureaucracy full of administrators. (2) The Keystone Kops do nuclear. (3) A government agency full of bureaucrats who couldn't competently oversee a popsicle stand who are put in charge of obscene amounts of nuclear material and nuclear weapons.

National Overhead Systems: See **national technical means.**

National Reconnaissance Office (NRO): (1) A big office with lots of pencils and bureaucrats. (2) The Keystone Kops due satellite spying.

National Security Council (NSC): A committee of high-level security and military officials whose main task is to dumb down security briefings given to the President.

national security: (1) Justification for whatever

unconstitutional or despicable activity a government agency or federal contractor is involved in. (2) Job security.

national technical means: A more politically correct, dishonest way of saying "satellite spying".

natural disaster: A storm, earthquake, flood, or wildfire that naturally turned into a complete disaster because of our lack of planning, preparation, and imagination.

need to know basis: See **need to know.**

need to know: (1) I have a badge (real, counterfeit, or expired). (2) Information absolutely essential to doing your job that nobody will share with you.

negligent security: (1) **due diligence**; (2) Your security if I got hurt or can pretend to be hurt.

nested security: Multiple layers of security, one inside another, none of which work.

netiquette: Cute, old-fashioned ideas about how to behave online.

Network Operations Center (NOC): The place where IT "doctors" do emergency operations that have to be performed on our sick network.

Network Security Administrator: A person who is

continuously conflicted about whether they are administering security or administering the network.

network sniffing: Trying to pinpoint that terrible smell coming from the cyber nerds in the **Network Operations Center**.

network sniffing: What your IT personnel are doing because of their cocaine habit.

next generation: Our components are so old, we can't buy them anymore.

noble cause corruption: Corruption

NOFORN: Self-evident, worthless information that cannot be released to foreign nationals without permission from the lunatic(s) who made it up.

non-disclosure agreement (NDA): The signee agrees not to share the worthless, ridiculous, or trivially self-evident information with anybody else that he obtains during a discussion or collaboration with a company.

non-repudiation: For whatever reason, we decide not to retaliate against an employee.

Notary Public: A person authorized by each state's Secretary of State whose main duty is to officially certify that they are a Notary Public.

nuclear containment: Packaging up hazardous nuclear materials so terrorists who steal it can transport it safely.

nuclear diversion: (1) Bored guards inside nuclear facilities play video games. (2) Nation-states take nuclear material from storage or nuclear material that was intended for peaceful purposes, and put it inside nuclear weapons without asking "Mother, may I?"

nuclear emergency support team (NEST): A group of nerds and bureaucrats who are scrambled during a nuclear emergency to do crowd control.

nuclear inspection: Looking busy.

nuclear inspectors: Persons with no meaningful background checks but who have diplomatic immunity who are allowed to poke around inside nuclear facilities.

nuclear material control and accountability (MC&A): An inventory system for nuclear material that is so devoid of security features and so utterly susceptible to spoofing that nobody can reasonably draw any meaningful conclusions about theft or diversion.

nuclear proliferation: Being in favor of nuclear liferation.

Nuclear Regulatory Commission (NRC): A government agency that makes sure nuclear power plants have enough fire extinguishers and bathrooms.

nuclear treaty obligations: Some nuclear stuff we would like your country to do or not do, if you feel like it.

nuclear weapons: What the 2nd Amendment gives you the right to personally own.

nuisance alarm: Any alarm just when the poker game was getting interesting.

obfuscation: Writing software code.

Official Use Only (OUO): Information that is only handed over to terrorists, criminals, scholars, journalists, or the Russians if you can get a receipt.

one-time pad = Vernam cipher: The only unbreakable cipher. Not much used because it isn't high-tech or cool enough.

one-time password: The password for a computer user who can't ever remember their password.

one-way mirror: See **two-way mirror.**

one-way turnstile: Hardware that allows bad guys to leave quietly after rummaging around the facility in order to avoid the threat of violence.

open source: (1) Software you wrote with the intent of letting the whole world see it so it can be improved. (2) Software you wrote that you didn't intend for the whole world to see but they have it anyway. (3) Information that is available to anybody, including sensitive and classified information.

optical bar code: See **bar code.**

optimizing security: Getting everybody involved a pay raise and/or shiny new technology to play with.

Our product has undergone extensive testing: It hasn't.

outsourcing: Hiring contractors who can be blamed when there is a security meltdown.

package control: A jockstrap.

pallet (skid): A platform or tray on which cargo is placed so that loading dock workers and cargo thieves can handle it efficiently as a single article.

pandemic: Everybody pans how bad our response to widespread infection is handled.

panic alarm: Any alarm.

panoramic camera: A video **surveillance camera** that gives 180° or 360° views with resolution such that it is impossible to make out any person or thing in the image.

parking the car: A man parks his car near a government building. A security guard comes up to him and says, "You can't park there! There are many important politicians who work here and often pass through here. The driver says, "Oh, there's no need to worry. I locked the doors."

passive infrared detector (PIR): A security device that doesn't do much except false alarm.

passive RFID: An **RFID** that doesn't do much except just sit there.

password protected: Not protected.

password: The string "12345678" or "password", the name of your spouse or pet, your birthday, or your zip code.

patent: A prank or demented submission to the U.S. patent office that was appallingly approved

Patriot Act: Um, you weren't actually serious about those Constitutional Rights, were you?

Payment Card Industry (PCI) Data Security Standard: A standard for how to handle credit card information that is frequently and wrongly claimed to mean we have good cyber security.

peer review: Subject matter experts and colleagues explain why your **security** sucks.

pen testing: (1) Playing around with our pen while the automated software looks for blatantly obvious cyber vulnerabilities. (2) A rigged security evaluation. (3) Superficially examining a small, unimaginative subset of possible attack scenarios while making various wrong assumptions, chief among them that the adversaries must be unresourceful morons and that there is no such thing as the **insider threat.**

perceptual blindness: (1) Our **security**. (2) Your boss.

performance appraisal: (1) A motivating factor for insider attacks. (2) A formal HR process that angers top performers and convinces poor performers that they might just as well slack off more.

perimeter patrol: Walking or driving along the fence line to try to compensate for our lousy perimeter security, fencing, and hardware.

perimeter security: Protecting the perimeter, because we sure as hell aren't going to be able to secure the interior.

periodic reinvestigation: We look for evidence—any evidence whatsoever—that we didn't make a colossal mistake in granting this guy a security clearance in the first place.

perjury: Lying to a court, Congress, or an official investigation that could theoretically get you in trouble, but really won't.

Personal Assurance Program (PAP): Critical employees with sensitive jobs are specially investigated to be sure than no journalists or taxpayers can find out that they are criminals, scumbags, terrorists, drug dealers, or psychopaths.

personal financial statement: Lies about money.

Personal Identification Number (PIN): A short, easily guessed sequence of numbers used for access purposes, typically 1234 or 1111.

Personally Identifiable Information (PII): Personal information about employees or customers, stored on unencrypted notebook computers left behind in coffee shops or unlocked private vehicles. Alternately, the same information, printed out on paper and then tossed in the organization's dumpsters.

Peter Principle: Every employee tends to rise to his maximum level of incompetence. From Prof. Laurence J. Peter.

phishing: Adversaries seek employees who are stupid, but not so stupid that they can't answer a question.

physical security: (1) Screwing up the protection of tangible, valuable assets. (2) Using physical means to screw up the protection of valuable intangible assets.

pickpocket: A federal contractor.

pilferage: Stealing medicine.

PIN: See **Personal Identification Number.**

PIR: See **passive infrared detector.**

plaintext: Writing that is dumbed down because the reader is an idiot.

plata o plomo **(lead or silver):** A saying in Mexico meaning "take a bribe or take a bullet".

plausible deniability: Just another day at the office.

police brutality: The policing tactic of first choice.

polygraph ("lie detector"): A device sort of invented by William Marston in the 1920's with about as much grounding in reality and science as his other major invention (Wonder Woman).

polygraph examiner: a charlatan, swindler, and/or science-denier, typically with less required training than required for certification to be a barber.

Post 9/11: The time period when we could all stop thinking profoundly about security.

post-it-note: A sticky piece of paper, attached to the computer monitor, where employees write their computer password.

post-traumatic stress disorder (PTSD): (1) A typical day at the office. (2) Being freaked out about where they posted you.

post-incident security review: Scapegoating after a security incident.

potentially unwanted applications (PUAs): All the software we write.

Power Over Ethernet (PoE): A connector that has to be consistently disconnected, then reconnected, in order to reset the Ethernet connection.

precursor: Potential warning signs that an employee might be planning an inside attack, or—on the other hand—might have gotten a new puppy, be planning a vacation, or attempting to refinance a mortgage.

pressure-sensitive adhesive label seal: See **Security Theater.**

prison guard: A security officer who protects the prison from vandalism by the locals.

privacy rights: Citizens and employees have a right to gripe about their loss of privacy.

private key: I humorously made up a key that is a string of obscenities and must now keep it secret to avoid getting in trouble.

private police: Police officers who refuse to respond to subpoenas.

private security: We have zero transparency and no accountability.

proactive security: We send around a lot of memos.

probable cause: It's likely we can make up an excuse for why we know the suspect is guilty as hell.

product anti-counterfeiting tag: Something a manufacturer or product counterfeiter places on a product to make the customer think it is authentic.

product counterfeiting: Our main concern is the safety of our customers. (Of course, the millions of dollars in lost sales are irrelevant.)

product tampering: (1) Well these things happen. (2) A nefarious act that the manufacturer denies after it happens.

professional conduct: The sleazy things you need to do to get money.

project: a boondoggle

project management: (1) Not a real thing. (2) Organizing a **project**.

promotion: See **Peter Principle.**

proprietary guard force: Our guards view their job as some kind of entitlement.

Protect and Serve: The motto and function of police officers, but only if allowed by the union.

protection officer: A cop or security officer who collects "protection" money from merchants and homeowners.

prox card reader: A plastic box mounted on the wall that sends a signal to open a locked door based on (1) a valid proximity card, (2) remote wireless signals from the bad guys, or (3) a voltage pulse from the bad guys' microelectronics that they hid inside the reader.

prox card: Security Theater on a plastic card.

pseudorandom number generator: Hardware or software that doesn't generate random numbers, but will repeat the sequence after a few thousand numbers.

public key: We can't keep the key secret so it's pretty much floating around among the general public.

public/private partnership: Both for-profit companies and government agencies are involved in this debacle.

QR code (Quick Response code): (1) A 2-dimensional bar code that take you to a fraudulent or dangerous web page, or uniquely identifies a product or counterfeit product. Called "Quick Response" because it is quick and easy for an adversary to copy or counterfeit the pattern. (2) A pattern you scan at the museum so that the listening device they rented you for $25 can play a pedantic description (in a fake English accent) of the museum artifact in front of you.

quality control: Bureaucratic mechanisms, procedures, and paperwork to prevent quality (or productivity) from ever happening.

quantum cryptography: Maybe quantum mechanics can make up for our utter lack of security.

******* R **

Rd Technique:** A method for questioning/interrogating employees that involves threatening, bullying, manipulating, accusing, and lying to the employee in hopes of getting a confession of some kind of wrong doing. Done because honesty and integrity is everything to our organization.

radiation badge: A passive radiation detector to tell you 30 days after the incident that you are in big trouble.

random number generator: Hardware or software that generates numbers that aren't random.

random procurement: Any procurement for government purposes.

ransomware: (1) Cyber geeks will provide you with the key to decrypt your hard disk if you promise never to write your awful software again. (2) What the hackers did after an attack to get away.

reactive security: security

real-time monitoring/intrusion alarm: (1) Our guard force ignores the evidence of nefarious activity immediately, rather than at a later time. (2) An easily blocked or jammed warning signal that MIGHT show up an hour or two after unauthorized intrusion.

real-time: True time, not the time you entered on your time sheet.

ReCAPTCHA: See **CAPTCHA**.

reception area: An official point of entry and egress for visitors, the use of which is preferred over all the other myriad ways the visitors can get in.

reciprocity: A mutual agreement between two government agencies to accept each other's insane, half-baked assessments of the degree of sensitivity for information in their possession.

recruiting more minorities and females: Attempting to hire more people from under-represented groups who have already sensibly concluded that they'd have to be stupid to work for your organization.

red team: (1) noun-A group of wise guys flagged for retaliation. (2) noun-The people that make our security managers turn red with embarrassment. (3) verb-Fooling around with a rigged "test" of your security by experimenting with one lame, blatantly obvious attack that the guards have been warned about.

redaction: Covering up confidential information with a black bar that can be easily removed.

reference: A friend or bribable person who will make up nice things to say about you.

regulatory requirement: Utter nonsense.

replay attack: Doing the same kind of attack over again because the security people never learn anything.

replay attack: Repeating an attack because the security manager learned nothing the last time.

residual risk: All our risk.

resilience: We're flexible as to whom we will name as the scapegoat(s) after the next serious security incident.

resiliency: Dodging the blame for all our security screwups.

reasonable person: A legal term that refers to people who are not lawyers, judges, plaintiffs, defendants, or jurors.

"resisting" arrest: Being a minority.

restricted area: A sensitive location where only authorized personnel are allowed, along with their friends, neighbors, family members, fellow gang members, drug dealer, and hired prostitutes.

retail security: Selling a low volume of security products at elevated prices.

return on investment (ROI): A fanciful argument about how all the money we have wasted (or want to waste) on bad security is somehow (absurdly) worth it.

reverse engineering: Trying to undo the mess the engineers have gotten us into.

RFID: An itty, bitty magical device that solves all security problems.

Risk Assessment: We list all the ways our security has failed us in the past.

risk executive: A high-level, senior manager who represents a huge risk to the organization, even more so than the other executives.

Risk Management: We collect all our wishful thinking, denial, and ignorance about security in one place, ideally accompanied by impressive looking matrices and lots of rankings/probabilities we made up.

risk: A security strategy where you take a chance that you can ignore threats and vulnerabilities such that the consequences will only show up after you retire or leave the organization.

robot security guard: A replacement for human security guards that is a lot smarter.

ROI (Return on Investment): The creative use of numbers to justify more funding.

role-based access control: An employee plays the role of a trustworthy employee in order to scam access.

roof: The entrance for burglars.

router: (1) Hardware that forwards malware to your network. (2) Easy hardware to tamper with.

RSA encryption: High-level encryption intended to (1) cover up the outrageous waste of company or taxpayer money that has been going on or (2) serve as a smokescreen for the fact that we have no meaningful security in place. The acronym stands for "Real Secret Asininity".

"Run, Hide, Fight": The mantra of security bureaucrats after bad security incidents occur.

***** **S** ***

safe: A small **vault**, differing only in the ease with which criminals and spies can walk off with it.

SAFETY Act: Legislation passed by Congress that lets you off the hook in terms of legal liability after a terrorist incident when the security products or services you sell turn out to be obvious crap.

safety expert: A safety subject matter expert who we rely on to run or help us understand security because we are confused about the difference between safety and security (plus safety is a whole lot easier).

sales engineer: A salesperson who doesn't understand the technology.

sanitization: Hiding information from the courts, the Inspector General, or history.

SANS Institute: Where we lock up former cyber security professionals who have been driven mad by the job.

Sarbanes-Oxley Act: Legislation passed in 2002 that specifies exactly how you should undertake your theft, embezzlement, and corruption.

scapegoats: The people arbitrarily selected for blame after a serious security incident. Typically chosen from among these 3 groups: those who had nothing to do with the incident, those who lacked the authority and resources to prevent it, and those whose warnings about the possibility of this or related incidents went unheeded.

SCIF (sensitive compartmented information facility): See **secure working area.**

SCRAM button: A button for emergency situations, always pressed too late.

seal database: An unsecured list of the **seal serial numbers** for the authentic or counterfeited tamper-indicating seals currently in use. May be used to check for tampering or unauthorized intrusion, if the seal inspectors feel like they have the time.

seal inspection: Looking busy.

seal serial number: A (sort of) unique number—which can be easily counterfeited--on a **tamper-indicating seal** that is sometimes checked to determine if there has been unauthorized access.

seal: See **tamper-indicating seal.**

search light: A bright light used to help find keys that guards dropped.

search or arrest warrant: A legal document that gives police officers the right to bust down the door and open fire at the wrong address.

secret: Our security procedures are such a joke, we have to keep them hidden out of sheer embarrassment.

secret agent: (1) Your idiot brother-in-law whom you managed to sneak onto the payroll without HR finding out about it. (2) The carcinogenic chemical they use every hour to keep the cafeteria clear of **COVID-19** virus.

secret compartmentalized information (SCI): Information that would be especially embarrassing or politically damaging if colleagues or the public found out about it.

secret operative: (1) See **secret agent**. (2) An adjective for something effective or essential that must therefore be kept secret from the auditors.

secret password: Any password that the user forgets because nobody can remember 16 gibberish characters.

Secret Service: (1) A specialized government agency who's contributions are unknown to the point where they might as well be secret. (2) Goofy guys in conservative suits, with swiveling heads and aviator sunglasses who stand out like a sore thumb in a crowd.

sectors: A cool-sounding word for "different parts of the building or facility".

secure shipment: An oxymoron.

secure working area (SWA): Starbucks.

secure: An abstract, unobtainable state.

security analyst: We aren't real sure what this person does, so we call him/her an "analyst".

security assurance: (1) We have reliable mechanisms in place to choose scapegoats when security incidents occur. (2) Confidence that we can BS about the five main **security goals**.

security audit / satisfy the auditors: We've pretty much given up trying to provide good security.

security auditor: (1) A mindless bureaucrat who doesn't understand security, is focused on minutiae, and thinks in advance that you are pond scum. (2) The only adversary that we need to worry about.

security award: An honor granted to anyone or any company that applies for it and pays the necessary fee.

security awareness training: Presentations that convince employees who once vaguely thought that security might be a good idea that they were sadly mistaken.

security badge: (a) A picture token that implies we have actual security because nothing else seems to suggest that.

(b) A computer-printed plastic card with a photo that looks nothing like you and with printing that cannot be read from a distance of 1 foot.

security by design: The crackpot idea that we should design buildings and facilities with security in mind, instead of just winging it, or applying security after the fact as a patch.

Security by Obscurity: A deliberate lack of transparency in security because ff the higher-ups or taxpayers found out how badly we are screwing up, they would be mad.

security career: One's permanent calling—at least until a position at the frozen yoghurt store opens up.

security certification: A designation granted to a security professional by a professional society, certifying that he or she is paying large sums of money to the professional society to keep the certification active.

security clearance: (1) Official authorization to rummage through classified information. (2) A credential automatically granted to relatives and friends of the President of the United States.

security conference sponsor: A company that has bought off the board of the organization running the conference.

security consultant: A BSing **consultant.**

Security Culture: (1) A petri dish full of pathological things. (2) Something we automatically say is critical for good security, but haven't bothered to think about or analyze.

security education: Education Theater.

security engineer: A **security technician** with a better title.

security expert: A person who, amazingly, has somehow managed to stay employed in security for a number of years.

security flaw: It's not a bug, it's a feature!

security gate: An official point of entry and egress in a fence or wall, the use of which is preferred over all the other holes in the fence or wall.

security goals: Often (erroneously) stated as confidentiality, availability, integrity, accountability, and assurance. In reality, the 5 goals are plausible deniability, scapegoating other people, looking busy, preserving your pension, and not taking a position on anything.

security guard rounds: (1) The number of sequential alcoholic drinks while on duty; (2) The number of bullets wasted while screwing around on duty.

security guard: (1) People we pay to play video games. (2) A felon. (3) An employee smarter than the people in charge.

security guru: A well-respected security practitioner who mumbles memorable adages and clichés.

security improvement: We spent more money.

security in depth: See **layered security.**

security incident: A security failure that the higher-ups or the press found out about.

security infraction: Poor security practice that did not result in a compromise of security as long as we don't look too closely.

security integrator: See **systems integrator.**

security level: A hierarchical ranking of the importance of various confidential or classified information, conveniently labeled so that the bad guys know what to concentrate on.

security lighting: Illumination that helps adversaries better see their target.

security management: (1) Marshaling, organizing, and coordinating inadequate resources and ineffective, unimaginative strategies against malicious attack. (2) See **management** (only more so).

security manager: (1) A person with no obvious

marketable skills, who takes credit for preventing imaginary attacks. (2) See **manager**.

security maxim: A simple-minded generalization thought up by someone who is simple-minded.

security markings: Markings, applied to sensitive documents indicating their security level ,that make things convenient for the bad guys.

security metrics: (1) Vanity metrics. (2) The creative use of numbers to justify more funding. (3) Made up numbers to make it look like we are doing something. (4) A quantitative measurement of how much busywork has been done in the name of security.

security mindset: Your mind is so rigidly set that you can't entertain new ideas about security.

security monitoring station: See **surveillance center**.

security myth: The basis of our **security** strategy.

security negligence: security

security officer training: Trying to get the knuckleheads to not put the uniform on backwards or to shoot each other.

security officer: Someone working in the security field who isn't well enough paid or treated with sufficient respect to be called a security professional.

Security Operations Center (SOC): The relaxation lounge
for our security personnel.

security perimeter: The boundary, inside of which there
isn't any real security.

security plan: Looking busy.

security policies: Fantasies about security.

Security Professional Code of Ethics: (1) A list of vague,
feel-good BS promises that security professionals pledge to
honor without reading. (2) A standard that security
vendors claim to honor while they are lying to you about
their products or services.

security professional: (1) Someone who won't let security
get in the way of doing his job. (2) A security amateur who
is well paid.

security question: Questions, the answer to which only
you could know such as, "What is the name of the person
you would like to lose your virginity to?" or "Exactly how
would you like to kill your boss?"

security requirements: Silly demands of our security
program, invented by clueless bureaucrats.

security research: Gathering or manufacturing data or
evidence that supports our pre-conceived notions or

practices.

security review: Desperately looking for any possible argument that our security is competent.

security salesperson: (1) Someone who hawks/hypes a security product or service who is even more evil than the adversaries for whom the product or service was ostensibly meant to neutralize. (2) The person we get most of our security information from.

security screw: (1) An oxymoron, referring to a screw with a special head that can confound some elementary school students (if they aren't very resourceful). (2) Fasteners designed to make it slightly more inconvenient for vandals to dismantle restroom hardware. (3) Your failure once again to get that security promotion. (4) A romantic rendezvous when a security guard is supposed to be on duty.

security standard: (1) A committee of special interests tries to legitimize bad practice and sloppy terminology through formal means. (2) Irrelevant BS.

security supervisor: A sociopath who couldn't hold down a real job.

security survey: Mindlessly wandering around with a pointless checklist for purposes of looking like you are actually on top of security (and to stretch your legs).

security technician: An hourly employee or contractor who used to work at one of those quick-change oil places or a sub sandwich shop.

security technology: Hardware and software for **Security Theater.**

security test: A rigged demonstration of **Security Theater.**

security testing: See **Security Theater**.

Security Theater: (1) Fake security for show. (2) Your security. (3) What keeps you employed in the security industry.

security thought leader: Somebody who is spouting off a lot of naive nonsense about security.

security tips: Mundane, self-evident security suggestions that are just the tip of the iceberg.

security use protocol: Specific details of how a security device or system is misused.

security vendor show: (1) A place to get free swag and win prizes. (2) A carnival for security people where they can be entertained by freaks, carnival barkers, snake oil, smoke & mirrors, and side shows.

security webinar: A 30- or 60-minute online

advertisement.

security: Various random, well-intentioned efforts by plodding professionals to protect people, buildings, information, and other valuable assets.

sedition: What the other political party does.

self-assessment: Self-serving motivated reasoning.

self-radicalization: The process undergone by a person who schemes to commit terrorist acts but is such a loser and screw-up that even terrorists want nothing to do with him.

sentry dog: A canine that is smarter than your human guards.

serialization: We assign (easily guessed) sequential serial numbers to each manufactured item because—really—we are totally coming up empty on any kind of serious anti-counterfeiting strategy.

sexually compromised: An employee's testicles got caught in the paper shredder.

shipper: (Confusingly) not who does the moving of cargo, but rather the party that wants shipping done.

shipping container lock: See **lock.**

shipping container: A thin-walled box with lots of holes that has been to countries that host terrorists and cargo thieves.

shoplifting: shopping

signals intelligence: Spying on US citizens.

smash and grab: (1) policing. (2) A government contract.

snake oil: See **security technology**.

SOCA: The Serious Organised Crime Agency in the UK. Not to be confused with the Silly Disorganised Crime Agency (SCCA).

social engineering: Something to warn employees about because an engineer who is being social is unusual and inherently suspicious.

social media site: An Internet location where employees go during working hours to upload sensitive and unflattering information about their work and employer.

socket: A plastic base for seating integrated circuits or microprocessors that make it easier for adversaries to tamper with electronics.

software code: Instructions for a computer, called "code" because nobody but the author can read it or understand what it means (and even he may not be able to).

software: Computer instructions that are soft on hackers.

software patches: 88% of what the average app is made of.

sound masking system: See **Cone of Silence**.

spam: Emails generated by anybody but you.

Special Access Program (SAP): (1) Efforts to limit access to special subsets of sensitive or classified information that would cause particular embarrassment if it became publicly known. (The acronym is indicative of the personnel enrolled in the program.)

special agent: A law enforcement officer or federal investigator who is called "special" because the word "retarded" is no longer politically correct.

spoofing: Fooling a security device, system, or program with things like duct tape and screwdrivers.

stairwells: Where we place **motion detectors**, even though intruders won't use the stairwells.

stakeholders: People who would drive a stake through our heart if they were fully aware of what we are up to.

stakeout: Hurry up and wait for investigators or detectives whose time isn't worth much.

stalker: Your ex.

stop & frisk: (1) Authorized sexual harassment. (2) A technique for antagonizing the local community so they become hostile to the police and won't therefore make so many **911** calls.

strategic plan: (1) A big picture analysis done every few years to keep managers busy that is irrelevant and out of date before the plan is printed; (2) Hilarious reading material for regular employees while sitting on the can.

stun gun: A frequently non-lethal weapon, used against anybody who isn't sufficiently deferential to a police officer.

subpoena: An official order to give testimony to a court or Congress, which you can ignore if you want to.

sudden changes in behavior: (1) An indicator that an employee might have become a risk for an insider attack. (2) What your significant other and most of your coworkers do regularly.

Supervisory Control and Data Acquisition (SCADA): A distributed video game for malicious computer hackers all over the world.

Supreme Court: 9 mediocre people of dubious character, ironically named "justices", wear silly robes while making arbitrary rulings based on their love of the rich and powerful, disdain for the Constitution, and personal political prejudices. Given a life-long appointment, they only have to "work" shortened banker's hours 9 months out of the year.

surveillance camera: (1) A video system with such poor resolution, you couldn't recognize your own mother. (2) A video system the guys rigged up to spy on the women's locker room.

surveillance center: (1) Lots of big screen TVs to entertain bored security guards. (2) Relaxation lounge for security officers and voyeurs.

SWAT Team: Gun nuts.

SWOT Analysis: Creating a table of a few of your or the organization's imaginary strengths, weaknesses, opportunities, and threats in order to avoid any serious self-introspection.

systems integrator: A vendor or contractor who somehow manages to wire all the security components together without tripping the circuit breakers.

***** **T** ***

tabletop exercise: (1) Play acting out your **Security Theater** plans. (2) A method for rehearsing your security response when it is too hot or cold or rainy to do it outside.

tag: Technology or intrinsic attributes used by the good guys or the bad guys to make it seem like the product, object, or container is unique and authentic.

tailgating/piggybacking: A frowned upon practice unless you are late for work.

tamper detection: Pretty much giving up on preventing the bad guys from entering.

tamper-evident label: A sticky label like kids enjoy that is a lot more fun and colorful than actual tamper detection.

tamper-evident packaging: A strategy for reducing jury awards when tampering inevitably happens.

tamper-indicating seal: (1) A security device that provides vague indications—but no proof—of unauthorized access, long after it happened. (2) A security device constantly confused with a lock, tag, real-time monitor, or O-ring.

tamper-proof seal: We and/or our customers don't really understand tamper detection.

tamper-resistant seal: We and/or our customers don't really understand tamper detection.

target hardening: Making buildings, facilities, and assets that are at risk of being attacked much harder for employees and the public to use.

team cohesiveness: The extent to which the employees with the truly good ideas are silenced and browbeaten.

teamwork: Everybody doing what the lunkhead in charge says.

technical excellence: Excellence only in a technical sense.

TEMPEST (Telecommunications Electronics Material Protected From Emanating Spurious Transmissions): Well, at least we tried.

terahertz security body scanner: Soft-core porn.

terrorism suspect: Some disturbed, maladjusted teenager who we entrapped into plotting a fake terrorist act that is too complex for him to otherwise manage, held up as an example of how effective our homeland security efforts are.

testing security: See **Security Theater**.

text analytics: Spying on employees' email and texts because what could possibly go wrong if employees feel disrespected, paranoid, creepy, violated, and are unable to vent?

theft of intellectual property: Being in business.

thermal imager (contactless thermometer): A device used to measure peoples' forehead skin temperature in order to identify who is sick and has not bothered to ice their forehead.

This is a security seal and this is an indicative seal: We and/or our customers don't really understand tamper detection.

threat actor: The bad guy analog of the good guys doing **Security Theater**.

threat assessment: An unedited list of bad guys we found after doing 10 minutes of research on the Internet.

threat matrix: Maybe if we put the superficially obvious in a table, along with random rankings and numbers, it will look profound.

throughput: The extent of meltdown in your access control plan that is required before you throw in the towel and declare that you are through with that equipment.

thumb drive: a miniature data storage device that when your employees find one in the parking lot, they plug it into their computer to see who it belongs to.

tilt, pan, and zoom: (1) The bored security guards are screwing around with the security cameras again. (2) What our security guards do when they show up to work drunk.

time expiring visitor badge: See **Security Theater** and **visitor badge.**

token: A physical electronic device used to validate a user's identity, called a "token" because that is all the security it provides.

top secret: Information that is even more embarrassing than our secret information.

track & trace: (1) A system for determining the fictious current and past locations of a product, counterfeit product, or stolen product, often a pharmaceutical. (2) See **Security Theater**.

trade secret: Business information well known to everybody in the industry and the Chinese government.

transportainer: A giant, unsecured sheet metal box that has been in countries that harbor terrorists and smugglers.

Transportation Security Administration (TSA): (1) See **Security Theater.** (2) A government agency that toggles between hiring airport screeners who are government employees and private contractors, depending on the latest security scandal.

Transportation Security: Making sure that the cargo is stolen at the truck stop, foreign port, or the destination airport, instead of in our facility.

Travel Advisories: Bored Department of State employees try to one-up each other to see who can come up with the scariest scenarios about what will happen to you if you visit safe countries.

travel reimbursement: Money you receive after official travel to cover drinks, gambling, and hookers.

treason: What the other political party does.

truck driver waiting area: A lounge at the warehouse, where truck drivers wait while their trailer is being loaded and can review the plan for the upcoming cargo heist.

TSA approved lock: The TSA certifies that this luggage lock offers no security whatsoever.

turnover: (1) The rate at which employees with insider information leave mad. (2) A metric for the old adage that people don't leave jobs, they leave jerks.

turnstile: Hardware designed to let only 1, 2, or 3 persons into sensitive areas simultaneously based on the credentials of one of them.

two factor authentication: You produce two different

things taken from this set to prove you should be granted
access: {something you have, something you know,
something you are, and something the bad guys know, have
or are.}

two-person rule: (1) A policy that sensitive work must be
overseen by two persons so that, out of fairness, the
proceeds from illegal or malicious activity doesn't go to just
one person. (2) A rule that makes inside attackers feel less
guilty about their wrongful acts because they can share the
proceeds with a friend.

two-way mirror: (1) A one-way mirror. (2) A mirror that
still works if turned upside down.

U.S. Space Force: The Keystone Kops go into space to
violate international treaties.

unauthorized disclosure: lunch

uniforms: Distinctive, unique clothing worn by our frontline security officers so that they can be distinguished from the other riff-raff who hang around the building.

unindicted coconspirator: (1) The top crook. (2) The President of the United States or a Cabinet member, member of Congress, Governor, or city councilman.

unique identifier: A technique or technology so lame, nobody else bothers with it.

unique seal serial number: There's less than a 50% chance that a seal in this order has the same serial number.

unprofessional conduct: A more skilled individual could have pulled off the corruption with a lot more finesse.

USB port: A female connector on a computer used for data transfer, malware insertion, and espionage. The acronym stands for "Undercut Security Badly".

vault: (1) A single room where all the valuables and sensitive/classified information are gathered so that adversaries can conveniently find it all in one place. (2) A fortified, large container that is either hardened so that adversaries may need a couple of extra minutes to gain entry, or else has real-time monitoring, which will cause security guards or the police to maybe show up a few hours after the alarm.

verification: A kind of **confirmation bias** where we look for superficial evidence that vaguely supports our preconceived notions or desired results.

veteran: A man or woman who courageously served their country but now receives 2nd-rate medical care.

Veteran's Day: A time that we honor the sacrifice of our veterans by diligently not getting the day off work.

video analysis: Turning fuzzy, shaky, out-of-focus, and/or poorly illuminated video into fuzzy, shaky, out-of-focus, and/or poorly illuminated video with much better color fidelity.

video recorder: A piece of junk that does low-resolution **video recording.**

video recording: Storing fuzzy, shaky, out-of-focus, and/or poorly illuminated video for later pointless analysis.

video surveillance camera: Security hardware that thieves like to steal and pawn.

video surveillance system: Big screen TVs to entertain bored security guards.

violent extremism: Shouting too loudly or flailing your arms around during a protest.

VIP (very important person): A high muckety-muck pougue who gets to bypass security because security is only for grunts.

virtual private network (VPN): A software tool that helps keep your computer safe by reducing your contact with the outside world via slowdowns and flaky computer behavior.

virtual reality: Our fanciful view of the actual security challenges.

virus checker: Software that scans your computer or network to determine if there are any really old viruses still present.

vision statement: A short summary of where our organization wants to go, put together by senior executives who fully understand that they will be long gone before anybody can hold them accountable for not making it happen.

vision: The ability to peer into the future and see a psychotic version of what we could be.

visitor badge: A computer-printed, paper or plastic sticker or card that saves the visitor the bother of having to counterfeit their own employee badge.

voice activated: Technology that ignores what you are saying even more than your spouse.

voice recognition: A technology for detecting when a person is angry, upset, or has a head cold based on the failure to recognize him or her, or what they have to say.

vulnerabilities: Things that don't exist.

vulnerability assessment: (1) A rubber stamp approval of our previous choice of security products, vendors, or strategies. (2) We found some guys who, for sufficient money, reported that no parts are missing. (3) A threat assessment where we are confused about the difference between threats and vulnerabilities.

vulnerability assessors: Wise-guy troublemakers who appreciate the value of nothing, especially hard work.

***** **W** ***

Walmart Effect: The rate of **shoplifting** decreases when a creepy senior citizen or character straight out of *Deliverance* greets you at the entrance. This is believed to work because it humanizes the store, gives the customer a sense that they are being watched, and makes them feel sorry for Walmart and all of humanity.

We stand behind our product: That's the only safe place to stand.

We use the _______ method for threat/vulnerability assessment: We'll pretty much go to any lengths to avoid thinking profoundly or creatively about security.

We want to follow a middle path between due diligence and paranoia: We don't want to hear about any #&!@!# vulnerabilities.

We will take these recommendations under advisement: We won't.

weapons of mass destruction: weapons

"What if?" exercises: Security professionals ask each other what it would be like to get a real job where you were treated with respect.

white supremacist: An uneducated, mentally-ill loser who still lives with his mother in the trailer park.

white team: The people who referee the phony engagement between the **red team** and the **blue team**.

whitelist: A list of emails or IP addresses whose maliciousness has not yet been recognized.

why programmers confuse Halloween with Christmas: Because 31 OCT = 25 DEC.

wireless alarm system: An alarm system where the burglars have yanked out the wires.

why crime is so low in Germany: It is against the law.

work and life balance: Good luck with that!

workplace violence: A typical day at the office.

***** **XYZ***

X-Ray screening: Making sure not too many x-rays are hitting the airport passengers at the security checkpoint.

zero-day attack: The time origin for the start of a new malware attack, designated as "zero-day" because we haven't actually thought about security prior to this time.

zombie: (1) A hacker-hijacked computer. (2) One of your security employees.

zones: A cool-sounding word for "different parts of the building or facility".

About the Author

Roger G. Johnston, Ph.D., CPP received his bachelor's degree from Carleton College, and M.S. and Ph.D. degrees in physics from the University of Colorado. He has won numerous awards, received 10 U.S. patents, authored over 200 papers and book chapters, and has given more than 100 invited talks in 10 countries.

Dr. Johnston is also the author of *Vulnerability Assessments: The Missing Manual for the Missing Link*, and the almost serious book, *Security Sound Bites: Important Ideas About Security from Smart-Ass, Dumb-Ass, and Kick-Ass Quotations.*